LORI SCHWEIGERT

MY LARGE WILD ANIMAL BOOK

ILLUSTRATED BY: Yvonne Abuda

CONTENTS

Black Bear   Brown Bear   Grizzly Bear

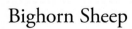

Bighorn Sheep   Bison

Elk   Moose

Kodiak Bear

Polar Bear

Caribou

Mule Deer

White-tailed Deer

Mountain Goat

Pronghorn

BLACK BEAR
(Ursus americanus)

Boar

Group
Sleuth or Sloth

The habitat of black bears is from Alaska, throughout Canada, into North America that goes as far south as Mexico. They are found in forested areas as well as in mountains and swamps.

Sow

Cub

The black bear is an omnivore eating mostly plants, roots, insects, and grubs. Honey is a favorite food. They will eat carrion.

BROWN BEAR
(Ursus arctos)

Boar

<u>Group</u>
Sleuth or Sloth
The habitat of brown bears ranges from forests to tundra to meadows to coastline. Their range is the northern parts of Alaska and Canada, Europe, and Asia.

Sow

Cub

Brown bears are omnivores. They
eat plants along with roots, fruit and
berries, and bugs. Fish, especially
salmon, are a favorite food as well as
honey. They also eat carrion.

7

GRIZZLY BEAR
(Ursus arctos horribilis)

Boar

<u>Group</u>
Sleuth or Sloth

The habitat of the grizzly bear is the mountainous and coastal regions of Alaska, northwestern Canada, and the northwestern corner of the United States.

(A subspecies of the Brown Bear)

Sow

Cub

Grizzly bears are omnivores eating
plants, roots, fruit and berries, bugs,
and fish, especially salmon, They,
too, will eat carrion.

KODIAK BEAR
(Ursus arctos middendorff)

Boar

Group
Sleuth or Sloth

Kodiak bear habitat is on the Kodiak Archipelago in southern Alaska. It ranges from the forests of the mountains to the rolling hills, tundra, and the coastline.

(A subspecies of the Brown Bear)

Sow

Cub

Kodiak bears are carnivores and omnivores. They eat fish, especially salmon, vegetation, seaweed, invertebrates, and carcasses.

POLAR BEAR
(Ursus maritimus)

Boar

Group
Sleuth or Sloth
The habitat for the polar bear is the ice sheets and costal waters of the arctic regions encircling the globe. This includes North America, Greenland, Norway, and Russia.

Sow

Cub

Polar bears are carnivores. They
like to eat seals, dead whales, dead
walruses, and bird eggs. Very seldom
will they eat plants.

BIGHORN SHEEP
(ovis canadensis)

Ram

<u>Group</u>
Flock or Herd

The habitat for bighorn sheep is in cooler climates on rocky cliffs. They range in the Rocky Mountains from southwestern Canada down to Baja California over to Arizona and east as far as North Dakota.

Ewe

Lamb

Bighorn sheep are ruminants so they
eat grasses and plants.

15

BISON
(Bison bison)

Bull

Group
Herd

Bison habitat consists of the open
grasslands and semiarid lands of North
America ranging from Alaska and western
Canada down to Mexico and east across
most of the United States. They especially
like the prairies, plains, and river valleys.

Cow

Calf

Bison will eat grasses, shrubs, herbs, and twigs.

CARIBOU
(*Rangifer tarandus*)

Bull

<u>Group</u>
Herd

The habitat of caribou is the northern colder regions of North America, Greenland, Europe, and Asia. They prefer to live by marshes, lakes, and rivers.

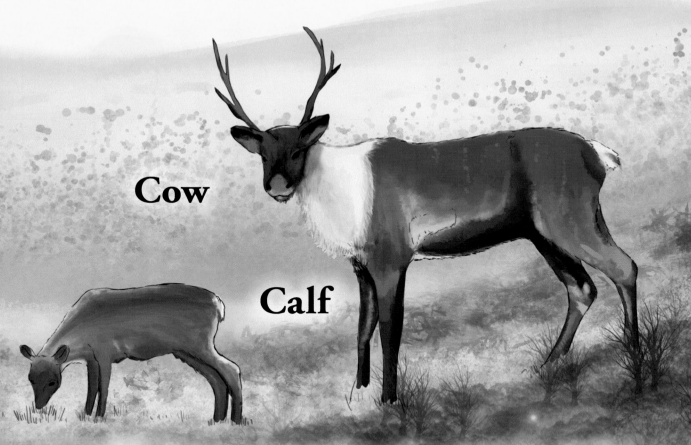

Cow

Calf

They have a summer diet and a winter diet. In the
summer, caribou will eat grasses and plants. In the
winter, they will eat lichen and mushroom.

MULE DEER
(odocoileus hemionus)

Buck or Stag

Group
Herd

The habitat of the mule deer ranges from forest edges of mountainous terrain to open plains and rocky hillsides in the western half of North America from costal Alaska south to Baja California and east to the Mississippi River.

Doe

Fawn

Mule deer feed on grasses, forbs, shrubs,
and trees as well as nuts and berries.

WHITE TAILED DEER
(odocoileus virginianus)

**Buck
or Stag**

Group
Herd

The habitat of the white tailed deer ranges from the forests and foothills of the mountains to fields, meadows, and river bottoms from southern Canada down to South America and from the Atlantic Ocean to the Pacific Ocean.

Doe

Fawn

They are herbivores so they eat
grasses, leaves, twigs, trees, fruits,
nuts, alfalfa, corn, lichen and fungi.

ELK
(Cervus canadenis)

Bull

Group
Herd or Gang
Elk habitat is mostly in the mountainous area of western to mid-western North America. They prefer to live in wooded regions.

(Also called WAPITI)

Cow

Calf

The food the elk eats is grass, tree bark, shrubs, and twigs.

MOOSE
(Alces alces)

Bull

Group
Herd

The habitat of moose is the marches, wetlands, rivers, and lakes of the subarctic to temperate regions of North America, Europe and Asia.

Cow

Calf

Moose have two diets. Their summer diet
consists of grasses, shrubs, and aquatic plants.
Their winter diet also includes shrubs and
they add pinecones, lichen, and moss to it.

MOUNTAIN GOAT
(Oreamnos americanus)

Billy

Group
Herd

The habitat of the mountain goat is on rocky cliffs in cooler climates. They live in the Rocky Mountains and the coastal ranges from Alaska through Canada down to Washington, Idaho, and Montana.

Nanny

Kid

Mountain goats eat grasses, flowering
plants, herbs, shrubs, sedges,
conifers, lichen, and mosses.

PRONGHORN
(Antilocapra americana)

Buck

Group
Herd

Pronghorn habitat is mostly the open ranges of North America, from southern Canada to northwestern Mexico and from the Rocky Mountains to the Great Plains states.

(Commonly called Antelope.)

Doe

Fawn

Pronghorns are herbivores. They eat grasses and other prairie plants, sagebrush, and forbs. They get most of their water from the plants they eat so they do not need to drink water very often.

Which animal am I?

Animal names

Black Bear

Kodiak Bear

Bison

Mule Deer

Moose

Brown Bear

Polar Bear

Caribou

White Tailed Deer

Pronghorn

Grizzly Bear

Bighorn Sheep

Mountain Goat

Elk

Vocabulary

Aquatic - plants or animals that live in the water most of the time

Archipelago - a body of water with many islands in it

Carcass - an animal's dead body

Carnivore - an animal that eats meat

Carrion - dead animals

Climate - the type of weather in an area

Conifer - trees with needles or scaly leave that makes cones

Forbs - a grass-like plant that flowers

Fungi - plants without flowers that live on and eat dead things; such as mushrooms, yeast, molds, and mildew

Habitat - what animals need to live: that arrangement of food, water, shelter, and space

Herbivore -an animal that eats plants

Herbs - types of plants used to give food flavor

Invertebrate - an animal that does not have a backbone

Lichen - a small plant that grows on rocks and walls

Moss - a green plant with small leaves that will grow on bark, rocks, or wet ground

Omnivore - an animal that eats both plants and animals

Ruminants - animals that eats plants and that re-eats their food

Sagebrush - a plant that grows in dry areas and smells like sage

Sedges - plants that live in wet ground

Semiarid - an area that gets little rain, a drier terrain

Subarctic - the area around the world just south of the Arctic Circle

Subspecies - a group of animals that belong to a species and have their own terrain to live in

Temperate - climate having temperatures that are not too hot or too cold

Terrain - a piece of land with its own layout

Tundra - treeless country that is mostly flat or with small rolling hills

Printed in the United States
By Bookmasters